Enjoy the book!

PAUL

Reesie *the* Blind Dachshund

A True Story

Written by P. G. Lachance   *Illustrated by* Leah Payne

Reesie the Blind Dachshund
Copyright © 2020 P. G. Lachance

ISBN: 978-1-63381-240-6

All rights reserved. No part of this book may be reproduced in any form or by any electronic or mechanical means, including information storage and retrieval systems, without permission in writing from the author, except by a reviewer, who may quote brief passages in review.

Illustrations by Leah Payne

Designed and produced by:
Maine Authors Publishing
12 High Street, Thomaston, Maine
www.maineauthorspublishing.com

Printed in the United States of America

For Sarah, Sawyer, and Hunter–
Reesie could not have found a better family.

Reesie was born in Louisiana.

We don't know much about that part of her life, but what we do know is that she ended up in an animal shelter and then eventually on a bus headed north.

After traveling many long miles, she spent her first night in a new shelter, close to our family in the state of Maine.

She had a lot of noisy neighbors who were also hoping to find a new home.

Momma fell in love with this scared little dachshund at first sight.

Our house was full, but Momma felt we had more room in our hearts, and she wanted to adopt a little dog. She made a trip to the animal shelter, and a shy little dachshund named Reesie simply stole her heart.

The kind person working at the desk said it would be best to take her home right away, just in case someone else came in and wanted to adopt her.

Momma really wanted to make sure her family was okay with it before she brought this sweet little dog home.

Most of the family loved the idea of adoption. Dad was still nervous about how a new family member would fit into their busy and full life.

Momma headed back to the shelter early the next day.

Unfortunately, someone ahead of her in line wanted to adopt Reesie! She just needed to introduce the little dachshund to her dog.

Momma was heartbroken. She told the helpful front-desk person she would be out in her car. Just in case.

Momma was sad. She went to her car and waited, not daring to hope.

Suddenly, the kind woman from the shelter tapped on her window. The other person had changed her mind about the adoption.

Reesie was still available!

Reesie moved into her new home with us on a wintry Maine day. She had probably never seen snow before. She did not like the icy weather, but it was warm in the house. She cozied up with her new family.

We were all very excited to meet her! Only Dad was still not sure how he felt about this new addition to the family.

Reesie began to settle into her new life. It did not take long for our family to realize that she was special. She did not behave like other dogs we knew. She didn't fetch or play, and she kept bumping into things.

Momma took Reesie to the veterinarian and told him, "We think Reesie may not be able to see very well."

The veterinarian waved his hands in front of Reesie's face and got no reaction. He checked her eyes. Reesie was mostly blind and would eventually lose all her sight.

That changed everything. We now understood why Reesie was different! Blind dogs need extra help. She would walk right into the cats. She could not go downstairs by herself.

Reesie loved being outside, but she could not go for walks like other dogs who could see. She ran into things.

Reesie needs help with some things, but there are so many things that she can do and enjoy on her own.

She loves to roll in the grass on a warm sunny day.

Reesie likes to run in safe places. The beach is her favorite even though she runs in circles.

Reesie loves to take naps on the couch. Dad gradually warmed up to Reesie and often takes naps with her.

Reesie is full of love and fits perfectly into our family. She loves to snuggle anywhere she can.

Reesie has lots of family and has made many friends.

She is a special dog and is very well loved.

When people first meet Reesie and learn she is blind, they often frown and say, "That is so sad!"

Reesie is not sad! She can feel the love around her and shares it back.

We are so happy that she joined our family.

The End.

About P. G. Lachance, and the inspiration behind *Reesie the Blind Dachshund*

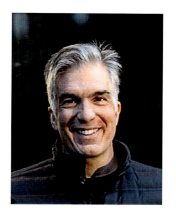

P. G. LACHANCE is a father, software entrepreneur, musician, and surfer living in Cape Porpoise, Maine. He has historically been on the busier side of life, and as he got a little older (and maybe a little wiser), one of the most helpful lessons he learned was to slow down and enjoy the simple pleasures around him each day. Reesie lives this way, and, as a dog, leads by example.

The author's sister, Gretchen, also blind, helped to share these day-to-day simple pleasures as well. He has written this book to honor both of them and to raise awareness and funding for Guiding Eyes for the Blind (GuidingEyes.org), a nonprofit organization dedicated to creating and supporting life-changing connections between blind people and dogs.

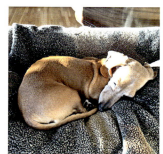    

For more information visit
www.facebook.com/ReesieTheBlindDachshund